CANCER

HOROSCOPE

2020

Cancer Horoscope

2020

Copyright © 2019 Mystic Cat

The images are used under license from Shutterstock, Dreamstime, or Deposit-photos.

Cancer

Cancer Dates: June 21 to July 22
Symbol: Crab
Element: Water
Planet: Moon
House: Fourth
Colors: Silver, white

JANUARY HOROSCOPE

ASTROLOGICAL & ZODIAC ENERGY

CURIOUS ~ ADVENTUROUS ~ VISIONARY

WORK & CAREER

You are ready to take on the world and bring new gameplay to light. Strutting your stuff, honing your talents, move you in a direction that offers you room to progress your creativity. It does nurture your abilities, giving you the place to grow and prosper. Opportunity favors the bold, your confidence is growing, bringing you options to expand your life. It does set the stage for an impressive journey ahead. You are set to benefit from a winning streak which helps you to overcome stumbling blocks, which have limited your full potential recently. Your dedication and perseverance to the task at hand, help you focus your energy with laser-beam accuracy. It does see you come out on top, and this has you find your groove, and make progress on your goals, as you awaken to a bounty of inspiration. You diverge from your usual routine and head off the beaten track, this enables you to discover a creative journey which helps develop your gifts further. It may lead to a new trajectory; it is a path that draws sustenance and abundance, allowing your sense of wellness to heighten. It creates a bold new beginning and sparks positive change. Laying the groundwork carefully provides you with secure foundations you can grow. It is time to prioritize your dreams and desires. You assert yourself with magnetism, it does bring mojo which propels your ability forward, it gives you progress on achieving personal goals. A moment to shine is ahead as you embrace the magic which surrounds your situation. Setting intentions for the path forward does bring qualities of manifestation into your world. The Friday the 10th Full moon in Cancer coincides with a lunar eclipse. This brings an emotional element into your life; it has you tapping into a deeper awareness around your working goals. It the critical month for plotting the course ahead; you plant the seedlings of aspirations, which blossom over the coming months. The lunar New Year occurs on the 25th of January, this is the Chinese year of the Rat, an auspicious year which offers you plenty of luck and good fortune in 2020.

LOVE & ROMANCE

Now is the time for the single Cancerian to create space to honor your feelings, and contemplate the path ahead. You are leaning towards a route that draws expansion and abundance; it does offer a bountiful way that removes limiting factors. This shifts you forward, it gets you back on track with following your heart and paying heed to your intuition. What is coming is definitely a positive shift forward for you. It is a theme of improving your circumstances while maintaining a steady course towards achieving your goals. This sees you enter a phase that offers golden moments; it is a path that can see you gain traction on a personal goal. It is also a time that has you dealing with some unfinished emotional sensitivity. Doing this healing work opens your life to exciting options. You are set to build strong support in your personal life, it is an excellent time to make an entrance into a community setting, this has you cross the path of someone who offers friendship and fresh ideas. A promising start soon follows; it does team you up with a new chapter of potential. Words are spoken from the heart unleash a wave of meaningful moments.

A secret is passed on to you through a mutual friend. This person has salacious information to share about your romantic partner, they can be a gossip, so be careful of what you reveal back to them. It does give you insight into a situation that had found itself cropping up in your life repeatedly. Paying attention to these types of patterns, let you spot a path forward. Your intuition guides you towards making a decision that shifts your focus forward. Change is moving your focus forward, it is a time which heightens options in your social life. It does bring exciting plans to light, which offers you a chance to mingle and enjoy life. This socializing is therapeutic, it nurtures your spirit, and provides you with a sense of renewal. It does bring good news; this is a gift you can embrace. Pouring your energy into your dreams draws results.

IDEAS & CREATIVITY

New energy arrives, it ushers in a clear path forward. Thinking about the possibilities, you discover a way to travel down, which fascinates, and it sparks your curiosity. It does see you focusing on an area that tempts you forward. This tantalizes and entices you out of your comfort zone. It creates a vital shift in your perception, broadening your view, you discover there is more potential seeking to emerge then previously noted. Fortune favors the bold. In this fantastic chapter, it brings options to light which are creative

5

and social, this draws a sense of connection into your world. If you have been feeling restless, this is guiding you to create space to nurture your life. It brings meaningful activities into your world and does it highlight a moment of bonding ahead that you can treasure. It is a boost that soon has you feeling more enthusiastic about the prospects. Improvement flows into your world, which draws stability. It does have you plotting a course towards achieving your larger goals. This creates an environment that nurtures abundance. The attention you bring towards organizing your life, does pay dividends, you enter a productive cycle, and this fortifies the foundations, it brings you to a turning point.

ISSUES & HURDLES

There is an emphasis on nurturing your life as you are ending a phase, there may be some healing and processing of emotions during this time. If you do feel more sensitive than usual, don't fight these feelings, create space to resolve, and release energy, which no longer serves your higher purpose. There is forgiveness of a situation or person ahead, this alleviates a great deal of heaviness which has been holding you back emotionally. It is a time for contemplation, introspection, and repose. An inner journey marks the beginning of a theme of self-development, which takes your emotional welfare further. It does see you pursuing areas that capture your imagination and provide you with a sense of connection and support. Signs and serendipity's are likely to make themselves known to you, it's all helping you access the right area which draws healing and abundance into your world. You are in a restful phase if your energy levels are low, it's a sign that you have depleted your reserves. It is a time of nurturing your spirit and creating space to spend time on a passion project. This can be something that draws happiness, but you often push to the side instead of other commitments. Making yourself a priority is precisely the recipe for success. It is an intense phase of following your heart and moving in alignment with your intuition. This expands your vision of what is possible for you this Chinese year of the Rat, which begins on the 25th of January.

FEBRUARY HOROSCOPE

ASTROLOGICAL THEME & ZODIAC ENERGY

SOULFUL ~ EFFECTIVE ~ ADAPTABLE

WORK & CAREER

The beginning of February is a time of steady progress for Cancerians in the workplace. Some gains are made, this gives you a strong indication of what can be achieved throughout this year. The first Supermoon for 2020 occurs in your sign on February 9th. This is the time to pause and reflect, if you have been going with the flow with your blinkers, things may be puttering along but if you feel that progress is lacking, open your eyes and see the broader picture of what is possible, it launches your potential into a league of its own. A bevy of opportunities exists on the outskirts of your life if you are willing to move out of your comfort zone. Keeping your mind focused on your long term goals does increase your ability to draw ambitious options into your life. It surrounds your situation with intelligent mentors and interested industry movers who are well connected. This brings new opportunities which heighten your career path and does mark a time that elevates your potential. There are untapped resources ready to be unearthed, your determination is your ticket to success. Being flexible, opening your heart to a broader landscape of possibilities, does draw stability into your world. Surrounding yourself with the right type of people, also gives you support, you can appreciate it. It does see you getting involved in learning a new area and sharing good times with people who celebrate your successes. If you have been thinking about shifting to an original path, now is the time to grow and evolve. You draw a line in the sand and step over to a new chapter. It does see you shifting to a path that is more in alignment with your long-term goals. This brings golden opportunities, it understands your situation blessed with a high rate of success. Making the right moves sets the tone ahead. It offers you a chance to grow your job. It's not a time to rush, the building blocks of your life demand stable foundations. Additionally, the new moon in Aquarius on the 23rd brings clarity. This information brings with it rejuvenating energy to help stabilize you over the Mercury retrograde phase.

LOVE & ROMANCE

Singles discover a secret arrives mid-month when you attract the attention of an admirer. This person does hope to build a stronger bond. They see you as someone refreshing, and the energy is fanciful, open, and curious. They haven't really made up their mind one way or the other, but they are leaning towards getting to know you on a deeper level. You have sparked their interest, and this is a situation that may blossom when nurtured appropriately. This person does see you as someone interesting. This person brings vital changes into your life, you gain a newfound appreciation for the journey which has been traveled over the last few years. You put into practice the wisdom you have achieved, it does give you a new approach to love, it brings a promising bond to light which hits a high point in your life. You form a connection with the one who sees your life flow more efficiently; it draws exciting moments to light.

The bonded Cancerian finds that their partner's commitment to the situation is blossoming. It is a time that sees a bond deepening. You are a loyal and dedicated person with vast powers of endurance, this brings practical abilities to develop long-term goals with one who inspires your mind. It does bring a new level of potential with this person. As the situation deepens, soul-stirring conversations bring fresh ideas. It sees you surrounding yourself in a more social environment soon with those who celebrate your success. This person has a tendency to be independent, they have a realistic approach to life and are immensely disciplined in their goals and dreams. You are someone they find fascinating, engaging, and enticing. It does see this person being pulled towards developing a closer bond with you. It is a path that is as rewarding as it is captivating.

IDEAS & CREATIVITY

During the February 9th Supermoon in Leo, you unwrap a cycle of new creative energy. Possibilities arrive to broaden your perspective, it does give you a unique array of options to contemplate. Revealing your right path rules a journey of personal growth, a long-forgotten dream arrives to tempt you towards nurturing your most sacred aspirations. It is a breathtaking, drawing abundance into your life, you harness a trailblazing stream of creativity and make progress on your goals. Brilliance is ready to illuminate your life with new potential. It's all part of a path of higher wisdom and learning, which is generating leads for you to spot. You may see symbols, coincidences, and other signs which guide your way forward. You are ready to move on and embrace a new state of being, revolution is shifting your focus forward towards an abundant journey of self-discovery. You enter uncharted waters soon, new potential shifts you're focused ahead. You embrace a forward-thinking chapter that inspires and motivates you to push back barriers, release restrictions, and enter a time of excitement and adventure. It does bring you avenues for growth, this kick starts a beautiful phase of harnessing the creativity within your intuition.

There is an impressive total of 4 supermoons in 2020. The more you tune into it, the more you are aware that you are going in the right direction. Your ideas blossom under the power of these supermoons.

ISSUES & HURDLES

This is a time where things feel unsettled, the sand is shifting, making you aware that things are changing, as you gain a foothold on a new area, you discover a need to go over old ground, fortify foundations, and re-stabilize your energy. Pulling back, creating space to nurture your life, is a valuable tool to draw equilibrium into your world. It does allow you to renew and rejuvenate your energy. Change is tempting you forward; it is a time where you can create distance from problematic areas. Putting them in the back window, shutting the door on a situation that feels done with, draws a line in the sand, it has you step over and enter a new chapter of potential. It does see you shifting the focus forward, new inspiration flows into your world, restoring balance. You reveal the cracks which have chipped away at your confidence recently, while this feels disconcerting, understanding there is a need to repair and solidify your foundations, does snap you out of the doldrums, it lets you deal with issues which are hindering your progress, and limiting your highest potential. It would serve you well to spend time anchoring your energy and grounding your situation as this draws renewal into your life.

Mercury retrograde this month can bring your energy down, as well. A secret is revealed, which brings you clarity about a disingenuous person. This person tends to be an enigma, one who answers only to themselves. Knowing that this person is a wolf in sheep's clothing does help you avoid disruption, it has you sidestepping potential hurdles before they negatively impact your life. Setting appropriate boundaries, putting up barriers where necessary, limits the detrimental effects.

9

MARCH HOROSCOPE

ASTROLOGICAL THEME & ZODIAC ENERGY

EXPERIENTIAL~ PROGRESSIVE ~ PERSISTENT

WORK & CAREER

The Full Moon in Virgo is another supermoon this month. As the season changes, so do your situation. It is an empowering time which heightens confidence, and pushes back boundaries, though it can drive up anxiety, you can deal with this expansion, approaching the path ahead gracefully, and taking things one step at a time, you face the future with an open heart, and this draws new adventures into your life. It lets you land in an area that feels spot-on for where you currently seeking to go. It is a busy time ahead, your schedule is filling up fast, this is an excellent time to organize, prioritize, and streamline commitments and obligations. Sifting and sorting through the areas which are demanding your time and energy enables you to release areas that cause the most considerable disruption. It helps you resolve conflict and gives you a solid direction to head down. Things are on an upswing as life picks up with a new pace soon. An area you pursue in earnest does draw benefit, it leads to inspiring ideas, and this offers you a great deal of motivation to develop the potential around your life. It brings new energy into this project of career-development. This sees you embarking on a path that simmers with golden opportunities to grow your abilities.

LOVE & ROMANCE

Singles find it is a time of essential change, it does see individual bonds shifting, and this can feel unsettling. As you move towards the busy season, there is a lot of social activity coming, it does bring opportunities to team up with your social environment, there is progress to be made by being flexible, and able to work on things harmoniously within the group. It does suggest a new goal coming, which you can tackle together. Widening your perception does elevate your situation, you begin to see things in a new light. There is abundance on the outskirts of your life, which is decidedly trying to emerge. It needs your open heart, your willingness to explore new horizons, and this is something which becomes a skill, the more you try to evolve your life, the easier it becomes. Life is a bounty of refreshing options that tempt you forward. Living by your truth sends a message clearly that you are a person of authenticity. Your idealism brings warmth to your world. It blesses your life with sunshine. There is an option to give back soon, helping others, being of service, brings opportunities that enrich your life.

Couples revisit an old stomping ground, life comes full circle, it reconnects you with the past. This does draw a sentimental theme through your world, it is a lovely trip through treasured memories. Focusing on where your heart lies, does draw abundance into your world. You enter an enchanting time when you discover the one who casts a spell on your life. Things come together, it brings a time which is fun and lively. You schedule in enough time to develop this situation by dialing back on other areas of your life. It does bring new energy into your life, and this person plays a central part in future events. It is a time that draws abundance and leaves you feeling content.

IDEAS & CREATIVITY

Things fully can come together for you, look for clues that guide you to a path of inspiration. You are entering a totally different cycle of potential, it does bring a whole new approach to life, and this elevates your potential. With the wisdom of hindsight, behind your vision, you have the confidence to spread your wings and appreciate a chapter of discovery. This eclipses the past and draws a happy vibe into your world. There is improvement coming into your life this month, this gives you a valuable signpost, it brings a new direction, and does leave you feeling more inspired about the potential possible in your life. If you have been feeling unsettled or anxious, this is set to be resolved as more positive news arrives. It does feel like a breath of fresh air, and this offers you a sense of renewal and rejuvenation.

ISSUES & HURDLE

Healing is a substantial aspect of the first part of March. Mercury retrograde ends on Monday 9th, and communication issues should improve soon after. It does also see the second super moon arriving on the same day. This full Moon in Virgo helps you tap into your emotional awareness. It brings you to a time of clearing away the blockages and letting go of outworn energy. It is a time which can feel sentimental, nostalgia makes an entrance turning your vision back to past events. This slows you down so that you can process the shifting sands of time, and integrate the memories into your heart which you treasure so dearly. It's also about creating space to nurture and grow your creativity. A vision arrives, which offers grace and wisdom. It does see you learning a valuable lesson, it brings insight into the past, turning the corner, you shut the door on an area which feels done with. A decision ahead gives you a comprehensive viewpoint from which to plan future goals. It does rebuild potential, drawing rejuvenation, and guiding you to a happier place. You are on a journey that takes your life further than you can currently envision. Becoming a catalyst of change, a strong focus on self-development takes you towards a path of healing. Peeling back the layers of your identity, you reveal you have inner strength and tenacity, which let you overcome hurdles. It is a time that puts you in touch with aspects of life that nurture your spirit.

APRIL HOROSCOPE

ASTROLOGICAL THEME & ZODIAC ENERGY

SUCCESSFUL ~ GUTSY ~ SKILLFUL

WORK & CAREER

You have been in a time of transformation, the Full Moon in Libra on 8th of April is a supermoon, it's also known as Hunters Moon, this delivers personal growth. You are gifted with a high degree of perseverance, tenacity, and resilience. You know how to overcome hurdles and stay the course until you achieve your chosen outcome. He admires your ability to crack the whip and get things done. It does enable you to progress your goals and come out on top. Welcome news arrives for you soon, this offers you a chance to advance your situation. It is part of a more extensive phase of growth; it leads to expanding your life and focusing on achieving a substantial goal. Your pioneering attitude blazes a path through new terrain. It is an empowering time where you can make a stellar result. Taking steps out of your usual routine initiates a positive trend of confidence and daring. It draws new opportunities that bring your vision further.

LOVE & ROMANCE

If things have felt restless on the romance front, the single and looking Cancerian can expect a new flow of energy to sweep when the supermoon in Libra occurs on the 8th of April. This incredible full moon helps shift things forward. You do have someone coming into your life, this is someone you've been destined to meet, there is a trajectory which draws you both together. Everything that has gone before has been a learning ground, it's provided you with the wisdom, the growth, and the insight necessary to spot the potential with this person. It's like, you might have not appreciated this person entirely had you not experienced everything else previously. This is the time which rules going after an area that inspires your heart. It is associated with forming a strong alliance with someone who brings joy into your life. Furthermore, the more you think about your goals, the higher your ability to fast track your dreams by utilizing the energy of manifestation.

13

The Cancerian is a relationship that finds that new information reaches you via a third party. This is seen as a revelation, it does uncover new data about an area which was previously hidden. Unearthing the dirt does bring clarity. It gives you a good idea about how things came about, and it also enables you to understand a situation better; this allows you to plan for a variety of contingencies. It does draw more stability into your world. Having this information helps you vibrate on a level that brings the situation closer. The energy you resonate reflects into your life in a more connected fashion. It does see your bond unfurling gently over time, you can appreciate the journey as much as the destination. Staying wide open to more connected potential does bring exciting news. It highlights the building of foundations, a promising chapter is ahead.

IDEAS & CREATIVITY

A long-forgotten dream makes an entrance into your life; it allows you to revisit an area that has been on the back burner for too long. This is something that creatively inspires; it sees you making progress this time around. Luck is on your side, it is the wind beneath your wings, enabling you to shift your focus forward and progress your dream. You touch down on new options soon, which inspires your mind and have you reaching further for your thoughts. Your enthusiasm is contagious, lively discussions see you sharing with others, and this provides you with bonding moments, your social circle fuels a more comprehensive phase of creativity, accessing the ideas which are shared, provide you with valuable insight into pathways of creative brilliance.

ISSUES & HURDLES

The Supermoon in Libra this month provides you with a prime time to release the past, letting go of resentments and frustrations resolves areas that have been holding you back. It is a time that brings endings, transitions, and change. It does touch your life on all levels, bringing changes to your personal life, friendships, and career path. Look carefully at the direction you are heading towards, make sure it serves your long-term goals and is in alignment with your personal truth. Things are shifting, and new people are likely to flow into your world soon. It is a time which launches your potential higher, it rules a trajectory of creativity, self-expression, and personal growth. Something you have been holding back from doing soon takes flight. It does remove the limiting factors and sees a breakthrough occurring, a meaningful exchange of ideas and thoughts bring new options into your life. Speaking the truth from your heart does take down the barriers. This is not a process that should be rushed and accept that healing does take time. It has taken many hurdles to diminish your energy to this degree, cleansing and purifying your energy during the Supermoon aids in creating space for the new potential to arrive soon afterward.

MAY HOROSCOPE

ASTROLOGICAL THEME & ZODIAC ENERGY

SPIRITED ~ TRIUMPHANT ~ IRREPRESSIBLE

WORK & CAREER

You're ready to kick off a chapter which is connected to pursuing your goals. You can soon initiate the development of an area that enables you to expand your dreams. Your approach to life is currently evolving, this allows your talents to shine, it leads to a change of mindset, one where you can feel more in control of the direction you are heading towards. Your life has undergone many changes, reinventing your situation is the perfect way to bring new energy into play. It does allow you to remove elements that no longer serve your purpose and stay focused on improving your situation by being flexible and adaptable to change. This is a time that draws abundance into your world, making the most of this chapter does see something of importance arrive. Look for signs that offer you a new path, it is the perfect time to bring something new into your life. It is a chapter of luck and good fortune, something exciting arrives, this is a high-level option which enables you to make progress on your larger goals. Maintaining the focus sees your determination and perseverance come out on top.

LOVE & ROMANCE

Singles can get ready for an exciting chapter, which offers you room to expand your horizons. You are willing to go the extra mile for people, your kindness and thoughtfulness allow you to shine. This draws abundance into your world, as you share your spirit with those around you, you discover a sense of purpose which stabilizes and surrounds your situation with blessings. Doing your part, being of service, is a vital way to nourish your soul. You are an incredible person with many gifts to share. This bodes well for your life, it does see options to circulate soon, your willingness to open your heart to new situations, draws the different types of people into your world. It aligns you to the path of abundance. Expect invitations to events as soon, which are vibrant and dynamic. This rejuvenates your spirit and is suitable for your soul. This is a time which draws options that delight, it is a memorable and tender chapter, there is much on offer, it is the perfect time to expand your life and look at areas which draw abundance. There is good news coming, this leads to some excitement in your house. You may be making some unique plans before long, and enjoy a bustle of new activity. It is time which offers social expansion, you are among warm and friendly people, this brings new friends. It is time spent well and blends perfectly with your future aspirations. Something you have been seeking is set to transpire, it gives you a good reason to feel excited about future potential. Things begin to come together nicely, giving you positive indications that you are on the right track to crack open a new chapter.

Couples this month find that there are opportunities to develop their romance. Things will come together over time, it is difficult when you have become emotionally invested in the outcome, and trying to unscramble mixed messages, can overcomplicate your life. Try to go with the flow and let a bounty of potential unfold naturally over time. You are set to improve your circumstances, the care and attention you bring to a situation of interest pay dividends. You enter new territory with a situation that is good for your soul. It does have you feeling this person is someone practical, yet artistic. This is someone who does things with flair, this person brings the right amount of thoughtfulness to the table. News arrives, which is upbeat, and you begin planning future ideas with this person. It does see a decisive leap forward occurring. Life becomes a whirlwind, and this draws abundance. You discover an opportunity to spend time in a social environment, this has you enjoying more of what life has to offer, you get to know the person who inspires your mind. It does blend beautifully with your personal goals, it gives you a chance to spend quality time speaking from the heart. You are particularly impressed with this person's authenticity, transparency, and openness. It provides a good indication that happiness is a byproduct of connection.

IDEAS & CREATIVITY

Reviewing your progress does bring insight into your current trajectory. Taking all elements into consideration, you may decide to diverge off the current path and explore an area that is more in alignment with your creativity. It does see you finding the perfect outlet for self-expression, this is a smart move, it has you drawing abundance and new opportunities into your life. It is the perfect partnership for your future aspirations. Old outworn layers of ideas will be shed so you can replenish your creativity. Releasing the past helps open your life up to new levels of potential. This is a process of letting and allowing for inspiration to flow into your life once more. Something that was blocking, muddying, and limiting your creative energy will be cleared. New beginnings ahead transform your outlook. Your perspective is changing towards a fresh start. You are ready to become inspired, enthusiastic, an open book – ready to be filled with new optimism. As you embark on this new journey of discovery, there is a sense of wonder filling your spirit, with untapped potential beneath your wings this month you, express openness, creativity, freedom, and independence

ISSUES & HURDLES

You have known troubles before, your resilience and tenacity are on the rise. Your patience and perseverance are rewarded, you discover soon, a prominent aspect which brings gifts and luck into your life. It is a good indication that happiness is just around the corner, do your part, stay open to new opportunities, and allow the passage of time to sail you into smoother waters. News arrives, which gives you a boost. You are ready to move away from sadness, something which has been holding you back is released, and this happens to lead to a personal breakthrough. It does take you to an avenue that offers more abundance, creativity, and self-expression. There is a good chance that staying open to new potential will bring you excellent options. It does show that you have unlimited potential, life comes full circle as you transition forward. The past has given you a new approach, it is taught you valuable lessons, you discover an entirely different way of dealing with issues. With the hindsight that has been gained, you begin to see the blessings in any challenges which crop up. It gives you a newfound appreciation for your ability to deal with life. Your wisdom is on the increase, stay tuned for a new avenue which grows your gifts further.

JUNE HOROSCOPE

ASTROLOGICAL THEME & ZODIAC ENERGY

EFFECTIVE ~ EFFICIENT ~ OBSERVANT

WORK & CAREER

As you shift your focus on achieving your goals, you are ready to rise up to the challenges ahead. It does see you drawing accolades, there is praise for work was done. This feedback gives you a greater sense of confidence, it motivates you to continue to set the bar high and go after your dreams. There is something in the pipeline, it's likely to be quite substantial, it grows your talents and expands your potential. This month sees exciting news is coming, it is a game-changing chapter, you are given room to expand your situation by focusing your energy on developing an area which captures your imagination. You have a natural knack for unveiling the highest potential possible in any given location. Mapping out new areas to explore, underscores your openness, your desire to benefit your case. You touch down on some enticing new options soon, this has you reaching for your dreams. It does see positive change arriving to tempt you towards pushing back boundaries and stepping out of your comfort zone. It is helping you achieve an impressive outcome, having a fixed goal in your mind, does see you taking the steps necessary to climb the ladder of success. A sunny aspect arrives to light a path forward. New adventures call your name, your wanderlust, and desire to branch out, bring new horizons. It does see a focus on an avenue that captures your interest. You begin to see a broader picture of what is possible when you make yourself a priority, fortune favors the bold, this sees your potential blossoming, it shines a light on a path which is refreshing and exciting.

LOVE & ROMANCE

You have attracted the attention of an admirer. Your personal magnetism is on the rise, this is drawing you closer to a situation which offers a crisp sense of chemistry. This person sees you as capable, alluring, and charming. It does have you noticing a sparkle that captures your awareness. This situation is never far from your mind, it is a time where you are expressly focused on developing a personal area. It does take you to an exciting chapter where you build your own life, it does see you connecting well with another, there is a lot of activity coming to your social life, it does shine a light on deepening a bond which helps you progress your dreams. A new friendship arrives to stir the pot, and this adds the spice of excitement to your life. It does see you brew up a storm, and add a pinch of manifestation to the mix. As you connect with the broader world of potential, you meet the one who sparks your interest, you discover a bond can be developed, this is a situation which fascinates you, it gives you a pleasant boost. It does take you by surprise, yet it comes together naturally and unfolds into something meaningful, this person complements your life, they bring a new zest to your spirit. There is improvement coming to your personal life. Following your heart leads to expansion, it revolutionizes your world and helps you connect with your soulmate. New foundations are built with an open and willing heart. You create a bond with an insightful person who opens the door to a happier chapter. It is an essential time of personal growth, and indeed, it draws the gift of stability into your world.

For the Cancerian in a relationship, a steamy romance with your love this month does grab your attention, the sweet part about this bond is the potential is quite substantial for something beautiful to emerge. It does position you towards developing a closer situation with one who inspires your heart. It sees things leading to a combination of chasing dreams and achieving a pleasing result. Open and honest, heartfelt communication lights a path forward. This is someone who supports your goals, their being in your life is a big plus, it gives you a chance to think big about the future, it does see you on a journey which is as valuable as a destination. Taking time to unfurl this potential, gently opens the gate to a happier environment. This is someone who enjoys the bond they share with you, they see you as someone adventurous and enticing.

IDEAS & CREATIVITY

You are feeling the residual effects of kundalini rising. It's all leading to an awakening where you make a breakthrough, you see clearly why your path is diverging, you are headed towards a quest of learning and growth. It does take you to the beaten track, you begin to focus more on the spiritual aspects, as you leave the mundane behind. You seek new experiences and embrace the breath of fresh air as an enticing new direction. It is a time where you make progress on a personal goal, this draws stability into your life, it brings you to a path that draws happiness and excitement into your world. As you embark on a new adventure, you stoke the fires of your inspiration, creativity is a critical element which provides solutions. Following your intuition and your heart brings brilliant ideas, and a yearning to expand your horizons draw a happier chapter. There are opportunities to connect with intuition and creativity ahead; this will help you tune into the signs from above, which do run through your life.

ISSUES & HURDLES

If you have been going through some turbulence, it is temporary, things are going to soon head towards an upswing. A creative idea you have is a winner, it does see you garner accolades. Staying conscious of your goals helps direct energy in a focused and brilliant fashion. You keep the fires of inspiration burning brightly and make progress on an area which offers room to progress your talents. Taking time to nurture your spirit transports healing energy to your mind, body, and spirit. It does set the scene for rejuvenation and draws peace into your world. As you rebalance your emotions, you pay attention to your closest ties, if there's been any area of your life which has been problematic, you discover a solution which enables you to talk with this person. It does see testing energy dissipating, abundance is ready to flow into your world. Creating space to pause and reflect does draw peace into your life. It considers the future shimmering with new potential, you emerge from your sanctuary feeling renewed and ready to take on the world. Your prospects are rising, this brings new options to explore. Troublesome energy is released; this allows you to focus on making progress. Something arrives, out of the blue, it feels like pure chance, but is perfect for your situation.

JULY HOROSCOPE

ASTROLOGICAL THEME & ZODIAC ENERGY

STIMULATING ~ DIRECTED ~ ADVENTUROUS

WORK & CAREER

Mercury retrograde ends on July 12th, the time is now ripe to go after your goals. Trusting the universe to support your expansion, you can take flight and seek a path that draws abundance into your life. You do find an area which stokes the fires of your imagination, this has you dreaming big about future goals, it does land you in an area which is ready for your talents. Expect a surprise to arrive soon. There lively indications that welcome news is going to light a path forward. It represents the fulfillment of a goal coming in your life, this releases limitations, your progress is no longer held back, as you reach a turning point, you're able to reshape your potential, and revolutionize your environment. This is a journey of abundance, stability, and security. It is a time which makes you smile, as you push back limitations, you expand your life and focus on the adventure of developing your dreams. This sees you stoking the fires of inspiration, as you move forward, you channel your enthusiasm and see the magic, which is possible when you focus your energy on achieving your goals. It does create impressive results, this propels you forward, and it suggests an active time of growth is ahead. News arrives, which sees you shift your focus towards a new project. Switching into manifestation mode, you create growth, and activate your innovative side, it does draw an option which lights a path towards abundance. Setting your sights on a lofty target, you see your vision growing through your attention to detail and your willingness to nurture your goals.

LOVE & ROMANCE

Singles can embrace a particular time; it does see more social opportunities arrive, which nurtures your soul. It is the perfect recipe for renewal, rejuvenation, and kicking back with your kindred spirits. An invitation to an event arrives, and this is extra special, you mark this in your calendar, and look forward to an exciting and vibrant time. There is plenty to be inspired about over the coming weeks, it is a time of abundance. There are some lovely changes set to flow into your life, something arrives, which makes you smile, it is going to let you step out of your ordinary routine and dive into a new area. The timing is ideal, this is a path which draws happiness and joy. It does show that your willingness to open your heart to a new level of potential does play a vital part in the events which unfold ahead. It is an enchanting chapter where you harness the magic within your spirit.

Information is revealed for the Cancerian in a relationship, this occurs at or soon after the Lunar Eclipse on July 5th, it gives you clarity about the situation with your love interest and with the end of the Mercury Retrograde phase this month, your romantic situation is set to blossom, your partner seeks a closer bond this month, there is a fascination with getting to know you better. It does suggest that you are likely to enter a chapter of getting to know this person on a deeper level. Your willingness to be open to change does see you staying on top of your game, you're in the box seat to progress your life, it is a time which supports growth as opportunities arrive that offer you a chance to develop your dreams. New potential opens the gateway, and an exciting option comes, this gives you something you can feel excited about exploring. You are ready to move forward, things are set to blossom in your world. This person is charismatic and intense, they possess deep emotions, due to their sensitive and perceptive nature, they give entirely when in love. Stability is essential to them, as they tend to ride an emotional rollercoaster during the vital phase of bonding. This person has a penchant for investigating the mysterious, spiritual, and divine. They see you as a person who is enchanting with bewitching charms.

IDEAS & CREATIVITY

A lunar eclipse combines with the full moon in Capricorn. This is the Wolf Moon, it may feel like an unsettling time where there have been many rapid changes, things are now headed towards a new path, it does bring you an enticing option. It is an emotional time where you slow down and integrate recent changes into your life. It may see you backtrack, looking at the past, and absorbing and reflecting on energy, which has been pushed to one side. Soon, forward progress is obtained when news arrives. Your realistic and pragmatic approach does set the scene to create tangible results. It is a time that sees your heart guiding you towards this new chapter of discovery. Developing this frontier sees you pushing back boundaries, expanding your limits, and focusing on an exciting stage of developing your dreams. This soothes the restless aspect of your spirit; it sets the stage for artistic growth and self-expression. As you reflect on the changes which currently surround your life, you will have a more significant epiphany of how much you have accomplished on your journey so far. A flood of inspiration returns into your world, and this takes you to a vibrant chapter which heralds abundant potential arriving to expand your horizons

ISSUES & HURDLES

Saturn makes an entrance on July 20th, this coincides with the new Moon in Cancer. The energy of the past is coming up, this enables you to reflect on what has gone before, it can bring up sensitive emotions, this is part of the healing process, it improves the stability possible in your world by enabling you time to process difficult emotions, and resolve outworn energy. It is a time that helps you cut away from the deadwood and embrace a new flow of potential soon. Setting your intention to heal is the first step, it does open your mind and your heart, it allows you to create space necessary to be open to change. It brings you to a more social environment. If you have limited your options, this is no longer going to hold you back, your confidence is rising. It is a time of taking stock, clearing your energy, and allowing the conditions to ripen. There is something special coming into your life; it makes you on a new journey of discovery, which is exciting and adventurous. A large social gathering is ahead, this provides you with a beautiful occasion to expand your wings and allow your dreams to take flight, it does connect you to those who inspire your mind.

AUGUST HOROSCOPE

ASTROLOGICAL THEME & ZODIAC ENERGY

COMMANDING ~ DECISIVE ~ INVENTIVE

WORK & CAREER

It is a good time for expansion, training a new role may lead to more options being unwrapped soon. It is a time which sees you making progress, you are ready to improve your bottom line, it does draw plenty of work opportunities your way. All kinds of good things are coming, it does see you making progress, life picks up speed, and it is the right time to make those plans for the future. Life is about to get busy, your focus will be on creating positive change, there are many aspects which require your full attention, this can feel like pressure, it does see some complexities which crop up, the dexterity of your mind soon finds adequate solutions. You are on top of your game, hitting your stride, and making substantial progress through an active chapter. It culminates in an offer that feels like a perfect fit. It is a difficult time, trying to negotiate a busy environment, does see you feeling drained, taking time to pace yourself, helps you make the most of this active chapter. Remain focused and strategic, and you can create fantastic progress on your situation. A new method that is applied draws a beautiful advantage. This helps you get the job done, and you soon start thinking about the next prospect on the horizon.

LOVE & ROMANCE

This month draws unexpected news for the single Cancerian, which brightens your life. A new friendship may blossom, its a time which does bring more opportunities to socialize, you find this is someone who introduces themselves confidently, and with the intent to getting to know you better. It does draw a lively conversation that sees a bond developing. It feels like it is a situation that can grow, encouraging feelings of kinship with this person has you feeling confident that this is something worth pursuing. After the difficulties of the past, you can embrace a chapter that is focused on harmony, excellent communication, and stable foundations. This person blends well with your zodiac sign, it is a good indication that things will work.

The Cancerian with a relationship sees that impressive results are likely to blaze through your personal life soon. This is a time that sees you focus on improving your romantic situation, as with all challenging crossroads, you may feel as though you are in a tug of war position. Taking time to heal unresolved energy, and settling your emotions will provide you with the foundations needed to make the correct choice. There is a situation which can feel up in the air, it may be experiencing some turbulence, and this will resolve in its own time. It does see an influence arriving, which draws more harmony into a bond. This brings goal-orientated growth, solutions are found, and it does make space for a more beautiful and comfortable situation to flourish. It is a time of overcoming obstacles and looking for practical and workable outcomes. It is a time that would serve you well to stay flexible, focused, and efficient. You can make progress by maintaining a steady course. There is a project which has been on the backburner, this finds a suitable outlet so you can move forward again. Your schedule is likely to fill up with new invitations, taking time to balance the busy chapter head helps you stay the course. You discover a compelling avenue, this soothes your restless spirit and gives you a new experience to enjoy. It does see a more relaxation and social environment emerging. It is a busy time, keeping organized with the invitations which crop up, does see you make the most of this active phase. Life is moving fast, there is much to do, and surprise news arrives to keep you on your toes.

IDEAS & CREATIVITY

You switch into manifestation mode when news arrives, which tempts you to shift your focus forward. This is a time of planning, and it does give you the motivation to start thinking about the future and opening the opportunities which are going to provide you with tangible progress. Your motivation is active, you can find ways to improve your situation. It is a time which puts your dreams front and center, having your energy be focused draws good fortune. An area you investigate offers a bumper crop. Your efforts are rewarded with an option that is loaded with potential. Unearthing this Avenue does inspire your mind. It feeds your spirit with new inspiration, this sees you moving in alignment with a path that draws abundance. It put you in direct contact with people who can improve your situation. Advancing a goal dear to your heart is an excellent motivator, seeing progress does wonder for your soul.

ISSUES & HURDLES

A secret is disclosed, which provides you with clarity about a situation that had ended poorly. If you've found there was a lack of closure around this situation, you now can resolve old energy and release the hurt by creating space to heal. It does see a transition occurring, this enables you to enter a new chapter, and it does have you feeling more confident about moving forward. The information learned draws new adventures. It does reconnect you with the past, life comes full circle, and this is to provide you with clarity into a previous situation. It enables you to reach the crossroads with the ability to make an informed decision about this person. The insight you gain is a valuable tool. You'll know in your heart when you've had enough, looking within, gaining insight into the problems which have been caused by this person enables you to take a step back and contemplate your options. You are facing a crossroads, it does see information being revealed soon, which help you make a firm decision. This does offer you a path that draws more abundance into your world. It is the first step of a powerful journey.

SEPTEMBER HOROSCOPE

ASTROLOGICAL THEME & ZODIAC ENERGY

DEPENDABLE ~ UNDERSTANDING ~ DURABLE

WORK & CAREER

A decision made at this time does crack open the potential possible. In short, it opens a gateway, and this sees fresh opportunity flow into your working life. It does shift your situation forward, moving out of your comfort zone does broaden your perception of what is possible. It could bring exciting news, your restless spirit is hungry for new experiences, and adventures, this all leads to growth. There is a lift which has a positive effect on your life, it does let you plant the seeds for growth, adopting the practice of flexibility, sees you maintain a steady course over the coming months. There is energizing activity arriving, which gives your career a boost. It does signify a celebration ahead, this brings a new tone into your life. The decision made at this time impacts future events, drawing abundance. You open new leads. It positioned you perfectly to explore a home-based business. It enables you to fortify and stabilize your prospects. This is a shift sideways that creates positive change and opens a gateway towards a happier environment. It's a time for dreaming, a sunny aspect is going to fling open the door to potential soon. As you lift the shutters on areas that have limited progress, you see positive signs that much is possible in the chapter ahead. It does directly align you towards advancement, this is a time of development where you can accomplish a robust result. It has you feeling proud and inspired.

LOVE & ROMANCE

Those who are single and looking for love, discover that their social life takes center stage, it illuminates new potential is possible by stepping back from your schedule to connect with a more social environment, in fact, this opens an intriguing pathway towards new possibilities. There is much to discover when you watch and wait. An invitation may arrive very soon; it inspires you to get involved in an area that draws abundance. It is a time which brilliantly lights a path forward, listening to your intuition does see things flow forward correctly. Improvement is coming; the pace noticeably picks up once you have created space to heal the past and have become ready to move forward. Things are set to become intriguing, a relationship started over the coming months does swiftly reach a high point, it is a windswept time, dreams become a reality and the glow of potential paints a marvelous hue over your life. It does see long-term plans becoming more evident, it involves focusing on developing a romantic situation that inspires your mind; it is an exciting chapter that brings the news you can celebrate.

This is a time where you feel encouraged to expand your horizons, it does see the fantastic development is possible, your star shines brilliantly, drawing new potential into your life. News arrives, which offers you an option that inspires your mind. This prospect is a giver of good fortune, it lands you in the ideal position to progress your goals. Other possibilities arrive to tempt you towards a more social environment. This is the time that influences your emotions, it gives you insight into the path ahead, it does involve deep conversations, good company, and social expansion. As you relax into this expansive month, you discover you can contemplate the path ahead with the luxury of having several options at your disposal. Moving alignment with your heart is always going to be the best call, a decision ahead tempts you forward. This is a lovely time of year for you, it is the bringer of gifts and good fortune, it puts you in an ideal position, as you garner the help of others and feel the support of your loved ones. It is a busy and social time, which sees your attraction rising, this brings news of something which gives your spirit a boost. A celebration is ahead, and there are lots to look forward to over the coming months.

IDEAS & CREATIVITY

This is a rare and curious time which sees new information revealed, as you move towards a new zone, you prepare to transition forward while keeping a sense of balance. Something you have been waiting for soon comes knocking, it does give you a positive indication that things are on the upswing. This leads to a more social time, which offers many blessings. It brings moments you treasure, and it is your time to shine. Your beautiful nature is ready to nurture a situation which blooms with your care and attention. You have abilities to create positive energy, this resonates in an ever-widening circle of abundance, you deeply touch those who are blessed to know you. The joy and abundance you resonate, rebound back into your life. This is a theme that is going to ring true over the coming season, it does take you to a lively path, and this hits the ticket for a chapter which draws happiness. You make some discoveries that broaden your horizons and take you to a broader world of opportunity. It does see a shift forward that integrates new options into your life. This leads to a happier chapter. It is a phase of reinvention, creating change inspires your mind, and this gives you an open path to explore, as exciting new adventures soon call your name.

ISSUES & HURDLES

If you get lost in your head by overthinking a situation, remind yourself to tune into your intuition and be fully aware of the decisions you are making around your life. Creating space to contemplate the path ahead can help clarify an issue that you may have been avoiding or been in denial about. It helps clear the fog and enables you to get valuable insight into the right path for your situation. It is a time where you downshift and reflect on the past. Processing events does help you take a break from drama, it resolves the stormy emotions and builds foundations that are more stable and resilient. If your intuition is sending nagging doubts, there is a need to clarify this situation, there may be an area that you have been avoiding, this mysterious tug on your awareness, is letting you know in no uncertain terms, you need to create the space necessary to root out and unearth something which is wanting to be found. Digging a little deeper does provide a breakthrough in this situation. It sets a tone of authenticity, which sees you setting the bar higher.

OCTOBER HOROSCOPE

ASTROLOGICAL THEME & ZODIAC ENERGY

IMAGINATIVE ~ EMPATHIC ~ AWARE

WORK & CAREER

News arrives, which is confidential, secret information, it shines a brilliant light which offers you a chance to progress your situation. It does bring an option to grow your dreams, it's not a quick fix, your perseverance and dedication are a vital element in achieving a long thought of goal. It does see your life becoming active and vibrant, motivation is running high, fueled by your hopes and aspirations. New energy is arriving, which draws a fresh chapter. It is a compelling path, you seek harmony and happiness, and go after your goals with a focused determination. Filtering out areas that no longer serve your higher purpose does help you move towards developing your working life in a more structured and practical manner. The past has given you wisdom, you harness the lessons learned and use them to create the change you are seeking. You're currently in a time of transition, this can feel unsettling, as one phase is ending, and the next source of inspiration is yet to begin, you may feel at a loose end, and wonder what the future holds. Creating space to explore new options does see a broad range of interests arrives to tempt you towards growth. You are ready for an original path of learning, it does show that something inspiring is set to blossom in your world.

LOVE & ROMANCE

Your personal life is set to move forward, it does see opportunities arriving which have you networking with an eclectic group of individuals. You show your passion and enthusiasm when lively discussions inspire your mind. Like energy attracts, and it does see you hitting a chord with someone you captures your attention. It's a time of social gold, new friendships emerge, and this may play an influential part in future events. Things are likely to shift forward for you, there is more focus on spending time with your friends, fun activities crop up which support a more active environment. This socializing is right for your soul, it brings you to a time of rejuvenation. It does see you recounting memories, a trip down memory lane hits a nostalgic note. This eases any burdens, it's a time of social abundance. There is some unusual activity likely to spark a wildfire of potential in your romantic life. It does see the end of a troublesome phase, and it gives you the power to create a more abundant environment. The decisions you make do support an aspect of personal growth. It emphasizes the development of romantic bond, this motivates you to embrace a more socially connected chapter, it does see exciting news arrive soon.

Cancerians in a relationship find that Mercury Retrograde delivers a bump in the road when it arrives on the 13th; you can navigate around it by being flexible. While Mercury Retrograde sees you reflecting on a situation that has left you feeling nostalgic, this contemplation allows you to gain a better understanding of how past events have brought you to this crossroads. A decision ahead does draw new options into your romantic life. It is a time of progressing your personal life and taking proactive steps to achieve your dreams with the one who inspires your heart. You have been restless recently, it is now time to embrace an exciting chapter of adventure and freedom. Currently, you are transitioning forwards, there is a shift taking place, which is seeking to create space to diverge your trajectory into new areas. Information arrives, which is a source of inspiration, it sets you on a path of exploration, your willingness to initiate growth is instrumental in revealing the full potential possible for your romantic situation.

IDEAS & CREATIVITY

You transition towards a significant event which is positive, but difficult in the short term. Mercury Retrogrades appearance creates a shift which requires strength, and fortitude. However, this blessing in disguise leads to a glorious outcome, you do discover a richly abundant path, heighten opportunities light a new journey forward. As the veil between worlds is thinning this month, you can notice more signs from spirit; it is an ideal opportunity to connect with those who have crossed over. This is a significant time where you can improve your circumstances. An area you develop initiates a wave of transformation which elevates your life on several levels. You will be pleased with the results. This is a time which rules communication, as the veil between worlds is shifting and becoming more transparent, you notice signs and interactions are abundant from those who are in spirit. You are surrounded by the energy of loved ones, and this does see your life slowing down, as you tear away from the demands on your time, and take a break to connect with your intuitive side. It is a time that brings a gentle flow of abundance.

ISSUES & HURDLES

There is a need for patience, balance, and perspective this month. It is essential to allow time for your creative ideas to germinate in the womb of your consciousness. Don't try to force or rush positive change in your life during the Mercury Retrograde phase, but gently guide this process forward. There is a situation in your life which has been problematic, reflecting upon the best course of action will help you make the correct choice. You may be searching for something which is going to take time to come together. Being flexible, taking a long-term view, broadening your perception of what is possible, does draw more stability into your life. You have faced stormy weather and grow stronger through your ability to navigate hurdles and come out on the other side. The wisdom you have obtained is priceless; you now can prepare to embrace some more extensive changes which draw abundance and ultimately take you towards a happier chapter. Part of this process is letting go, moving away from the past, to create space for new potential. Life holds a refreshing change for you soon. It is a time that draws movement and discovery; on the basis of this, it is an active cycle that is leading you towards new horizons. You tap into a sense of excitement and adventure, embarking with an open heart, you draw new potential into your life. It does see you reaching for your dreams, and discovering an area which glimmers with promise. You are ready to open a new book of exciting chapters. It's all about achieving those long-dreamed-of goals and fighting those battles which see you come out on top and achieve your desired outcome. Happiness appears radiantly on the horizon; you seek your destination and track a path towards an environment that glimmers with new potential. Forward motion next month is going to shift your focus towards achieving a pleasing result.

NOVEMBER HOROSCOPE

ASTROLOGICAL THEME & ZODIAC ENERGY

IDEALISTIC ~ ENERGETIC ~ VISIONARY

WORK & CAREER

Information is coming, which sparks your curiosity, it does see the new potential is set to blossom in your life. It is a time that drives your talents further as you embark on developing a passion project which offers room to grow your skills. This is a time which provides hidden gems, it sees your success rate flourish, as you blaze a trail towards achieving your dreams. You have beautiful gifts which are going to help improve your situation. An opportunity comes knocking, and it does spark your interest. A new endeavor or project is likely to cross your path, as you contemplate the steps necessary to make the most of this opportunity, you realize you can head towards growth, and go after your dreams. It is also a month that sees many demands upon your time at work. There are added pressures, a hectic environment, and an increased workload indicated. You have the skills needed in which to handle this situation effectively, and you're able to maintain equilibrium without getting overly stressed. Focus on the most critical tasks first, and maintain a sense of balance by being mindful not to focus too heavily on one area or another. Spreading your energy around, and delegating tasks when possible, will allow you to keep the momentum moving forward. As you deal with the various demands around you at work this month, keep your focus on staying balanced, and continuing to move forward, you will enjoy the benefits of increased productivity this month.

LOVE & ROMANCE

Singles discover that this is a time which may draw a new admirer, it does heighten your confidence, this attraction feels irresistible. It does have a sense of magnetism and synchronicity, which is bringing two people together. Socializing as much as possible does see this come together nicely. It attracts good company, lively conversations, and this sees you striking while the iron is hot, as friendship blossoms. If you have doubted the potential of your love life, and if it would improve, meeting this person reminds you that the universe does fill the void. You have done extraordinary work, you've raised the bar, and removed the deadwood which was limiting your progress. Creating space for something new does see fresh opportunities entering your life. This secret admirer is hoping for the right opportunity to develop a closer bond with you. This person is keeping their eagle eye on potential events or parties you may be attending over the coming months. This is someone who feels that timing needs to be right, they want things to develop naturally, they are afraid of appearing awkward or nervous. It does seem that the potential in your personal life is likely to move forward. You are blessed with a fierce heart that knows no boundaries. While this can see you giving freely to those who may take advantage of your good nature, someone is coming who is going to recognize themselves in your spirit. It does mark a bold new beginning; it is a path of transparency, authenticity, and loyalty. This is someone who understands what it is that you seek, a bond forged through sharing profound experiences together.

Those in a relationship find that flexibility and compassion bring balance into the equation. The stability is secured through a greater understanding of what each other needs. You are drawn to expressing yourself openly in love and romance with loving acts of kindness. This giving creates a beneficial karmic effect in your life, as it inspires and encourages your love interest to give back to the relationship. In giving, you end up receiving gifts of honor, prosperity, harmony, and love. You are encouraged to be open and radiate the love that comes from deep within you. This is a time of emotional peace, stability, and equilibrium for you. Feelings of contentment abound, and that gives you renewed confidence that you are on the right path to developing your personal life correctly. Overall this month suggests an improvement in circumstances surrounding your love life. As you spend time visualizing potential outcomes, it helps clear a path which encourages the powers of manifestation in the realm of love

IDEAS & CREATIVITY

Something new is on the way for you; there is a creative element that blends perfectly with your artistic side. There is terrific energy arriving to boost your spirit, and this captures your imagination. It is a more active time, you thrive in this busy environment, and enjoy the hectic pace ahead. It does light the way forward and provides you with an outlet which is industrious, yet also social. Life picks up momentum soon, it helps you reshape your goals, as you draw a more social environment into your life. It leads to a chapter filled with abundance and magic, there is a beautiful theme surrounding your situation, which has you expanding your horizons, and becoming more open to new friendships. Spending quality time with like-minded people sets foundations, which restore equilibrium. You are ready to open the door to a fresh start, it marks a bold new beginning, there is surprising news on the horizon, which can lead to an expansive chapter. It does see you get involved with an area which is likely to be ideal, you can embrace this abundant influence which is currently emerging, by following your heart, and giving your dreams a chance to unfurl. Several options are arriving to tempt you towards a new avenue. Information is coming, which highlights an expansive chapter; it is a sign that you are ready to create space for something new to blossom. Gaining traction on your goals leaves you feeling motivated and inspired, you can bank on this enthusiasm, as it is going to take you places.

ISSUES & HURDLES

The problematic energy eases as Mercury Retrograde ends on the 3rd. However, it may leave you feeling unsettled, anxious, and a sense of disquiet. So much of this month is about working on your inner garden. It is a time of finding your way out of the maze of confusion that Mercury Retrograde has left in its fuzzy wake, by solving the mystery of your melancholy, you will unlock the puzzle and gain access to your happiness. It is a month of personal discovery as you walk your own path towards the renewal of spirit. However, this inner work is not easy, and it's hard to face that which causes you emotional pain. Tuning into the sympathetic vibrations of the universal unconscious helps you see the bigger picture, and allows for your consciousness to merge with the divine. Spending time under the darkness of New Moon this month, will aide in healing emotional wounds, and as you absorb the lunar power of the darkest moon, you will be guided towards intuitive insights. Look for secret symbols to help guide your paths, such as moon-shaped symbols, or recurring numbers or patterns. These symbols are guiding you towards a deeper intuitive understanding and will help heal you and protect you during this personal process of healing and cleansing your energy. The New Moon is also a valuable ally that provides you with a time of gentle grace where that which feels comfortable in the darkness can emerge to be safely acknowledged. You heal hidden aspects of yourself by accepting and understanding their presence, allows this your energy to be renewed once the moon grows into it's a full lantern on the 30th.

DECEMBER HOROSCOPE

ASTROLOGICAL THEME & ZODIAC ENERGY

TRADITIONAL ~ EXCITING ~ HECTIC

WORK & CAREER

You are entering a vital time relating to your career path. It does suggest a professional opportunity is arriving soon, this gives you a fantastic reward for the work you have undertaken this year. This is a time that represents new beginnings, opportunities, and potential. This impacts your life on many levels. An unexpected opportunity may come your way, and this gives you something to feel inspired about. It is a highly energetic month, which unfolds creatively and does offer you a myriad of options to explore. It is such a significant time that you can embrace the beneficial events which follow. There is an influx of creativity coming into your world. This puts you in a stellar position of being able to create solid plans for future progress. It opens the door to a direction that inspires your mind and motivates you to expand your horizons. It is a landmark time that takes you further and represents an increasing sense of freedom and independence. You release restrictions that have kept you feeling limited in the past. Being adept and flexible brings a valuable reward. It opens your horizons, which let new people and experiences past your barriers and into your life. It takes you to a chapter of exciting adventures. You have grown a great deal through overcoming past hurdles, your wisdom and experience can now be beautifully utilized to draw substantial benefits into your world.

LOVE & ROMANCE

December does look promising for those who are single and looking for love, it's bound to put you in contact with some fascinating people who offer you the chance to collaborate on an area which is sturdy and stirs your inspiration. December sees you being involved in a more social phase. Soon, mingling with others will prove to be enlightening. There's no doubt about it, change is in the air, the new potential is coursing through your life, lighting up the areas of creativity, passion, and self-expression. A flurry of activity coming to your life soon. This does amp up potential and enables you to shift towards a more vibrant and social chapter. It may throw your energy out at first, so taking the time to rebalance and integrate the demands on your time will provide you with a stable foundation from which to launch your expansion. It is a curious time that delivers a wonderful boost to your personal goals.

Those in a relationship see a new theme is going to resonate through your life over the coming month. This brings excitement to the forefront of your awareness. Growth is ready to come knocking; it leads to an expansive chapter that brings you great joy. As you embark on a productive cycle, you can gear up for improvement in your circumstances, it shifts your dynamics favorably forward and lights up the potential for trips away. You are intent on improving your conditions, this favors expansion in your social sector, it does highlight specific invitations arriving for you soon, which offer relaxed get-togethers. Sharing vivid conversations with others could see an old drama resurface, if this happens, don't rehash old wounds. There is a moment with your love interest, which offers a significant turning point; it does highlight an influx of fortuitous energy arriving, which stimulates growth, and it turns the focus towards planning for next year.

IDEAS & CREATIVITY

December is a month that provides you with heightened creative powers. You are ready to pull the trigger and unleash a new chapter into your world. You are someone who can harness a positive outlook and utilize your inherent sense of optimism to lead towards a new avenue, ready to be explored. It is a time of magic possibilities, as a new cycle of change is unfolding. Your thoughts are manifesting goals, which, in turn, become a progression of actions that you undertake to achieve the desired results. You are bold and creative this December. You channel your energy into a project which represents strength and power. You use dormant skills, but after brushing them up, you find that you can develop them further. You influence others with your integrity and compassion. It is a time that expands and rejuvenates your spirit as you put yourself out there and make a bold and decisive move forwards. A new possibility opens up, which puts your mind at ease; you begin to see clearly how much can be accomplished during this ambitious chapter. March does see you pursue your ideas; this relates to developing a new area of growth. It is a pet creative project which gives birth to a flurry of inspirational ideas that help it grow. You are ready to take a risk and make a bold move forward to make your dreams a reality.

ISSUES & HURDLES

There is an undercurrent of transformation occurring in your life, the year is complete, it has been eventful, it has been a journey into growth and learning. You are given space during the solstice on the 21st to reflect on the difficulties you have faced, and how you rebalanced your emotions, you find that life you can better control your feelings and accept what life throws at you without becoming destabilized. An emotionally balanced and calm approach enables you to face challenges head-on and manage situations logically. Your intuition also provides you with a depth of understanding of others' personalities; this comes in handy for you soon. It's a month that portrays transformation and significant change ahead for you. This enables you to release a situation that has been problematic and formulate goals and dreams from the ground up. After a period of reflection, you release an aspect of your life, which is no longer serving your higher purpose. Closing one door leads to a new gateway being opened. Parting ways with a situation sees that you are ready to embrace new opportunities and possibilities.

ASTROLOGICAL DIARY

2020

Astrological Diary

2020

Time is set to Coordinated Universal Time Zone (UT±0)

January

Mon 30

Tues 31

Wed 1
New Year's Day

Thurs 2

January

Fri 3

First Quarter Moon in Aries. 4.45 UTC
Quadrantids Meteor Shower. Jan 1st-5th. Peaks night of Jan 3rd.

Sat 4

Sun 5

Notes

Lucky Numbers: 11, 62, 12, 61, 32, 5
Astrological Energy: Experiential
Color: White

January

Mon 6

Tues 7

Wed 8

Thurs 9

January

Fri 10

Full Moon in Cancer. Wolf Moon. 19:21 UTC
Penumbral Lunar Eclipse.

Sat 11

Sun 12

Notes

Lucky Numbers: 23, 30, 22, 15, 27, 11
Astrological Energy: Directed
Color: Bone

January

Mon 13

Tues 14

Wed 15

Thurs 16

January

Fri 17
Last Quarter Moon in Libra. 12.58 UTC

Sat 18

Sun 19

Notes
Lucky Numbers: 32, 88, 26, 40, 92, 85
Astrological Energy: Optimistic
Color: Sky Blue

January

Mon 20
Martin Luther King Day

Tues 21

Wed 22

Thurs 23

January

Fri 24
New Moon in Capricorn. 21:42 UTC

Sat 25
Chinese New Year (Rat)

Sun 26
Last Quarter Moon in Scorpio. 21.10 UTC

Notes
Lucky Numbers: 27, 95, 10, 77, 23, 2
Astrological Energy: Visionary
Color: Indigo

January

Mon 27

Tues 28

Weds 29

Thurs 30

Fri 31

Sat 1
Imbolc

Sun 2
First Quarter Moon in Taurus. 1.42 UTC.
Groundhog Day

Notes
Lucky Numbers: 80, 11, 88, 22, 68, 99
Astrological Energy: Influential
Color: Violet

February

Mon 3

Tues 4

Weds 5

Thurs 6

February

Fri 7

Sat 8

Sun 9

Full Moon in Leo, Supermoon. Snow Moon. 7:33 UTC

Notes

Lucky Numbers: 31, 16, 96, 44, 21, 26
Astrological Energy: Commanding
Color: Midnight Blue

February

Mon 10
Mercury at largest Eastern Elongation.

Tues 11

Weds 12

Thurs 13

February

Fri 14

Valentine's Day

Sat 15

Last Quarter Moon in Scorpio. 22.17 UTC

Sun 16

Notes

Lucky Numbers: 93, 70, 24, 17, 39, 52
Astrological Energy: Imaginative
Color: Royal Blue

February

Mon 17
Presidents' Day

Tues 18
Mercury Retrograde begins

Weds 19

Thurs 20

February

Fri 21

Sat 22

Sun 23
New Moon in Aquarius. 15:32 UTC

Notes
Lucky Numbers: 49, 52, 8, 43, 85, 76
Astrological Energy: Adventurous
Color: Gold

February

Mon 24

Tues 25

Shrove Tuesday (Mardi Gras)

Weds 26

Ash Wednesday

Thurs 27

February/March

Fri 28

Sat 29

Sun 1

Notes

Lucky Numbers: 24, 67, 64, 94, 96, 55
Astrological Energy: Vivacious
Color: Yellow

March

Mon 2

First Quarter Moon in Gemini. 19.57 UTC

Tues 3

Weds 4

Thurs 5

March

Fri 6

Sat 7

Sun 8

Notes

Lucky Numbers: 84, 50, 93, 9, 48, 8
Astrological Energy: Productive
Color: Hot Pink

March

Mon 9

Full Moon in Virgo, Supermoon. Worm Moon. 17:48 UTC
Mercury Retrograde ends.
Purim (begins at sundown)

Tues 10

Purim (ends at sundown)

Weds 11

Thurs 12

March

Fri 13

Sat 14

Sun 15

Notes

Lucky Numbers: 27, 62, 37, 49, 90, 69
Astrological Energy: Passionate
Color: Cyan

March

Mon 16

Last Quarter Moon in Sagittarius. 9.34 UTC

Tues 17

St Patrick's Day

Wed 18

Thurs 19

March

Fri 20

Ostara/Spring Equinox. 3:50 UTC

Sat 21

Sun 22

Notes

Lucky Numbers: 74, 38, 95, 88, 2, 72
Astrological Energy: Constructive
Color: Spring Green

March

Mon 23

Tues 24

Mercury at most substantial Western Elongation.
Venus at most substantial Eastern Elongation.
New Moon in Aries. 9:28 UTC

Weds 25

Thurs 26

March

Fri 27

Sat 28

Sun 29

Notes

Lucky Numbers: 3, 93, 58, 91, 27, 81
Astrological Energy: Trusting
Color: Rose

Mon 30

Tues 31

Weds 1

First Quarter Moon in Cancer. 10.21 UTC
All Fools/April Fools Day

Thurs 2

April

Fri 3

Sat 4

Sun 5
Palm Sunday

Notes
Lucky Numbers: 3, 66, 5, 74, 53, 82
Astrological Energy: Celebratory
Color: Lemon

April

Mon 6

Tues 7

Weds 8
Full Moon in Libra, Supermoon. Pink Moon. 2:35 UTC
Passover (begins at sunset)

Thurs 9

April

Fri 10
Good Friday

Sat 11

Sun 12
Easter Sunday

Notes
Lucky Numbers: 86, 33, 34, 35, 75, 61
Astrological Energy: Harmonious
Color: Amber

April

Mon 13

Tues 14

Last Quarter Moon in Capricorn. 22.56 UTC

Weds 15

Thurs 16

Passover ends

April

Fri 17

Orthodox Good Friday

Sat 18

Sun 19

Orthodox Easter

Notes

Lucky Numbers: 37, 65, 90, 62, 99, 5
Astrological Energy: Inspiring
Color: Baby Blue

April

Mon 20

Tues 21

Weds 22

Lyrids Meteor Shower. April 16th-25th. Peaks night of April 22nd.
Earth Day

Thurs 23

New Moon in Taurus. 2:26 UTC
Ramadan Begins

April

Fri 24

Sat 25

Sun 26

Notes

Lucky Numbers: 88, 39, 83, 85, 26, 28
Astrological Energy: Committed
Color: Honeydew

April

Mon 27

Tues 28

Weds 29

Thurs 30
First Quarter Moon in Leo. 20.38 UTC

May

Fri 1

Beltane/May Day

Sat 2

Sun 3

Notes

Lucky Numbers: 18, 15, 51, 13, 41, 1
Astrological Energy: Complex
Color: Deep Pink

May

Mon 4

Tues 5

Weds 6

Eta Aquarids Meteor Shower. April 19th - May 28th. Peaks night of May 6th.

Thurs 7

Full Moon in Scorpio, Supermoon. Flower Moon. 10:45 UTC

May

Fri 8

Sat 9

Sun 10
Mother's Day

Notes
Lucky Numbers: 43, 65, 59, 5, 54, 34
Astrological Energy: Productive
Color: Forest Green

May

Mon 11

Tues 12

Weds 13

Thurs 14

Last Quarter Moon in Aquarius. 14.03 UTC

May

Fri 15

Sat 16

Sun 17

Notes

Lucky Numbers: 11, 68, 9, 39, 20, 88
Astrological Energy: Vibrant
Color: Aqua

May

Mon 18

Victoria Day (Canada)

Tues 19

Weds 20

Thurs 21

May

Fri 22
New Moon in Taurus. 17:39 UTC

Sat 23
Ramadan Ends

Sun 24

Notes
Lucky Numbers: 81, 34, 21, 97, 66, 43
Astrological Energy: Courageous
Color: Dark Violet

May

Mon 25
Memorial Day

Tues 26

Weds 27

Thurs 28
Shavuot (begins at sunset)

May

Fri 29

Sat 30

First Quarter Moon in Virgo. 3.30 UTC
Shavuot (ends at sunset)

Sun 31

Notes

Lucky Numbers: 29, 85, 92, 91, 60, 30
Astrological Energy: Complex
Color: Slate Blue

June

Mon 1

Tues 2

Weds 3

Thurs 4

Mercury at Greatest Eastern Elongation.

June

Fri 5

Full Moon in Sagittarius. Strawberry Moon. 19:12 UTC
Penumbral Lunar Eclipse.

Sat 6

Sun 7

Notes

Lucky Numbers: 74, 57, 56, 75, 67, 33
Astrological Energy: Daring
Color: Straw

June

Mon 8

Tues 9

Weds 10

Jupiter at Opposition.

Thurs 11

June

Fri 12

Sat 13
Last Quarter Moon in Pisces. 6.24 UTC

Sun 14
Flag Day

Notes
Lucky Numbers: 24, 61, 96, 42, 88, 47
Astrological Energy: Active
Color: Fire Brick

June

Mon 15

Tues 16

Weds 17
Mercury Retrograde begins.

Thurs 18

June

Fri 19

Sat 20

Sun 21

New Moon in Cancer. 6:41 UTC
Midsummer/Litha Solstice. 21:44 UTC
Annual Solar Eclipse.
Father's Day

Notes

Lucky Numbers: 21, 96, 92, 61, 36, 70
Astrological Energy: Exciting
Color: Cornflower Blue

June

Mon 22

Tues 23

Weds 24

Thurs 25

June

Fri 26

Sat 27

Sun 28
First Quarter Moon in Libra. 8.16 UTC

Notes
Lucky Numbers: 5, 91, 69, 39, 64, 6
Astrological Energy: Creative
Color: Red

June/July

Mon 29

Tues 30

Weds 1
Canada Day

Thurs 2

July

Fri 3
Independence Day (observed)

Sat 4
Independence Day

Sun 5
Full Moon in Capricorn. Buck Moon 4:44 UTC
Penumbral Lunar Eclipse.

Notes
Lucky Numbers: 58, 40, 99, 95, 18, 92
Astrological Energy: Curious
Color: Orange

July

Mon 6

Tues 7

Weds 8

Thurs 9

July

Fri 10

Sat 11

Sun 12

Last Quarter Moon in Aries. 23.29 UTC
Mercury Retrograde ends.

Notes

Lucky Numbers: 7, 36, 2, 20, 98 77
Astrological Energy: Stimulating
Color: Crimson

.

July

Mon 13

Tues 14

Jupiter at Opposition.

Weds 15

Thurs 16

July

Fri 17

Sat 18

Sun 19

Notes

Lucky Numbers: 82, 42, 66, 87, 42, 58
Astrological Energy: Inventive
Color: Ruby

July

Mon 20

New Moon in Cancer. 17:33 UTC
Saturn at Opposition.

Tues 21

Weds 22

Mercury at Greatest Western Elongation.

Thurs 23

July

Fri 24

Sat 25

Sun 26

Notes

Lucky Numbers: 31, 46, 25, 23, 43, 37
Astrological Energy: Methodical
Color: Peach

July/August

Mon 27

First Quarter Moon in Scorpio. 12.32 UTC

Tues 28

Delta Aquarids Meteor Shower. July 12th – Aug 23rd. Peaks night of July 28th.

Weds 29

Thurs 30

July/August

Fri 31

Sat 1

Lammas/Lughnasadh

Sun 2

Notes

Lucky Numbers: 35, 1, 7, 53, 26, 51
Astrological Energy: Constructive
Color: Lavender

August

Mon 3
Full Moon in Aquarius. Sturgeon Moon. 15:59 UTC

Tue 4

Wed 5

Thurs 6

August

Fri 7

Sat 8

Sun 9

Notes

Lucky Numbers: 30, 76, 90, 8, 41, 21
Astrological Energy: Independent
Color: Scarlet

August

Mon 10

Tues 11

Last Quarter Moon in Taurus. 16.45 UTC.

Weds 12

Perseids Meteor Shower. July 17th to August 24th. Peaks night of Aug 12th.

Thurs 13

Venus at Greatest Western Elongation.

August

Fri 14

Sat 15

Sun 16

Notes

Lucky Numbers: 65, 36, 98, 86, 47, 9
Astrological Energy: Aware
Color: Bronze

August

Mon 17

Tues 18

Weds 19
New Moon in Leo. 2:41 UTC

Thurs 20
Islamic New Year

August

Fri 21

Sat 22

Sun 23

Notes

Lucky Numbers: 40, 33, 63, 37, 45, 56
Astrological Energy: Spirited
Color: Mint

August

Mon 24

Tues 25

First Quarter Moon in Scorpio. 17.58 UTC

Weds 26

Thurs 27

August

Fri 28

Sat 29

Sun 30

Notes

Lucky Numbers: 22, 1, 30, 25, 2, 6
Astrological Energy: Enchanting
Color: Turquoise

August/September

Mon 31

Tues 1

Weds 2

Full Moon in Pisces. Full Corn Moon. 5:22 UTC

Thurs 3

September

Fri 4

Sat 5

Sun 6

Notes

Lucky Numbers: 86, 69, 78, 50, 71, 80
Astrological Energy: Unique
Color: Topaz

September

Mon 7
Labor Day

Tues 8

Weds 9

Thurs 10
Last Quarter Moon in Gemini. 9.26 UTC

September

Fri 11
Neptune at Opposition.

Sat 12

Sun 13

Notes
Lucky Numbers: 10, 12, 38, 62, 13, 91
Astrological Energy: Magnetic
Color: Coral

September

Mon 14

Tues 15

Weds 16

Thurs 17
New Moon in Virgo. 11:00 UTC

September

Fri 18

Rosh Hashanah (begins at sunset)

Sat 19

Sun 20

Rosh Hashanah (ends at sunset)

Notes

Lucky Numbers: 1, 54, 36, 80, 79, 57
Astrological Energy: Open
Color: White

September

Mon 21
International Day of Peace

Tues 22
Mabon/Fall Equinox. 13:31 UTC

Weds 23

Thurs 24
First Quarter Moon in Capricorn. 1.55 UTC

September

Fri 25

Sat 26

Sun 27

Yom Kippur (begins at sunset)

Notes

Lucky Numbers: 53, 89, 92, 97, 79, 71
Astrological Energy: Magical
Color: Maroon

September/October

Mon 28
Yom Kippur (ends at sunset)

Tues 29

Weds 30

Thurs 1
Full Moon in Aries. Harvest Moon. 21:05 UTC
Mercury at Greatest Eastern Elongation.

October

Fri 2
Sukkot (begins at sunset)

Sat 3

Sun 4

Notes
Lucky Numbers: 42, 11, 26, 5, 82, 14
Astrological Energy: Empathic
Color: Dark Orange

October

Mon 5

Tues 6

Weds 7

Draconids Meteor Shower. Oct 6th-10th. Peak night of Oct 7th.

Thurs 8

October

Fri 9

Sukkot (ends at sunset)

Sat 10

Last Quarter Moon in Cancer. 0.39 UTC

Sun 11

Notes

Lucky Numbers: 64, 1, 59, 48, 36, 61
Astrological Energy: Organized
Color: Chocolate

October

Mon 12

Columbus Day
Thanksgiving Day (Canada)
Indigenous People's Day

Tues 13

Mercury Retrograde begins.

Weds 14

Thurs 15

October

Fri 16
New Moon in Libra. 19:31 UTC

Sat 17

Sun 18

Notes
Lucky Numbers: 49, 37, 22, 78, 8, 4
Astrological Energy: Perceptive
Color: Salmon

October

Mon 19

Tues 20

Weds 21

Orionids Meteor Shower. Oct 2nd - Nov 7th. Peaks night of Nov 21st.

Thurs 22

October

Fri 23

First Quarter Moon in Capricorn. 13.23 UTC

Sat 24

Sun 25

Notes

Lucky Numbers: 96, 91, 20, 27, 33, 76
Astrological Energy: Mysterious
Color: Black

October

Mon 26

Tues 27

Weds 28

Thurs 29

Fri 30

Sat 31

Full Moon, Blue Moon in Taurus. Hunters Moon. 14:49 UTC
Uranus at Opposition.
Samhain/Halloween.

Sun 1

All Saints' Day

Notes

Lucky Numbers: 50, 44, 49, 97, 25, 1
Astrological Energy: Psychic
Color: Midnight

November

Mon 2

Tues 3
Mercury Retrograde ends.

Weds 4
Taurids Meteor Shower. Sept 7th - Dec 10th. Peaks on Nov 4th.

Thurs 5

November

Fri 6

Sat 7

Sun 8

Last Quarter Moon in Leo. 13.46 UTC

Notes

Lucky Numbers: 43, 18, 73, 51, 54, 92
Astrological Energy: Profound
Color: Royal Blue

November

Mon 9

Tues 10

Weds 11

Remembrance Day (Canada)
Veterans Day

Thurs 12

November

Fri 13

Sat 14

Sun 15
New Moon in Scorpio. 5:07 UTC

Notes
Lucky Numbers: 10, 7, 54, 57, 91, 21
Astrological Energy: Hectic
Color: Teal

November

Mon 16

Tues 17

Leonids Meteor Shower. Nov 6th-30th. Peaks night of Nov 17th.

Weds 18

Thurs 19

November

Fri 20

Sat 21

Sun 22

First Quarter Moon in Pisces. 4.45 UTC

Notes

Lucky Numbers: 75, 92, 5, 47, 99, 93
Astrological Energy: Structured
Color: Sky Blue

November

Mon 23

Tues 24

Weds 25

Thurs 26
Thanksgiving Day (US)

November

Fri 27

Sat 28

Sun 29

Notes

Lucky Numbers: 7, 25, 52, 75, 67, 55
Astrological Energy: Social
Color: Magenta

Mon 30
Full Moon in Gemini. Beaver Moon. 9:30 UTC
Penumbral Lunar Eclipse.

Tues 1

Weds 2

Thurs 3

December

Fri 4

Sat 5

Sun 6

Notes

Lucky Numbers: 87, 3, 92, 14, 83, 13
Astrological Energy: Impulsive
Color: Midnight Blue

December

Mon 7

Tues 8

Last Quarter Moon in Virgo. 0.37 UTC

Weds 9

Thurs 10

Hanukkah (begins at sunset)

December

Fri 11

Sat 12

Sun 13

Geminids Meteor Shower. Dec 7th-17th. Peaks nights of Dec 13th-15th.

Notes

Lucky Numbers: 67, 10, 7, 43, 76, 99
Astrological Energy: Vibrant
Color: Snow

December

Mon 14
New Moon in Sagittarius. 16:17 UTC

Tues 15

Weds 16

Thurs 17

December

Fri 18
Hanukkah (ends at sunset)

Sat 19

Sun 20

Notes
Lucky Numbers: 16, 85, 10, 96, 67, 1
Astrological Energy: Festive
Color: Powder Blue

December

Mon 21

Ursids Meteor Shower. Dec 17th – 25th. Peaks night of Dec 21st.
Great Conjunction of Jupiter and Saturn.
Yule/ Winter Solstice. 10:02 UTC
First Quarter Moon in Pisces. 23.41 UTC

Tues 22

Weds 23

Thurs 24

December

Fri 25
Christmas Day

Sat 26
Boxing Day (Canada & Uk)
Kwanzaa begins

Sun 27

Notes
Lucky Numbers: 33, 6, 30, 17, 80, 76
Astrological Energy: Graceful
Color: White

December

Mon 28

Tues 29

Weds 30
Full Moon in Cancer. Cold Moon. 3:28 UTC

Thurs 31
New Year's Eve

January

Fri 1
New Year's Day
Kwanzaa ends

Sat 2

Sun 3

Notes
Lucky Numbers: 23, 15, 12, 29, 71, 86
Astrological Energy: Aware
Color: Green Yellow

May the stars shine brightly in your world in 2020 and beyond.

About Crystal Sky

Crystal is passionate about the universe, helping others, and personal development. Crystal produces a range of astrologically minded diaries to celebrate the universal forces which affect us all. All reviews are read and appreciated.

Other Titles in the 2020 range:

Fairy Moon Diary 2020: Fairy Messages & Astrological Datebook
Shaman Moon Diary 2020: Shamanic Messages & Astrological Datebook

When not writing about the stars, you can find Crystal under them, gazing up at the abundance that surrounds us all, with her dog by her side.